T F

MW01697777

TODAY GOD IS FIRST

Group Bible Study

by Os Hillman

ASLAN GROUP
PUBLISHING

Printed in the United States of America

ISBN 1-888582-08-1

Marketplace Leaders/Aslan Group Publishing
3520 Habersham Club Drive
Cumming, Georgia 30041 USA
678-455-6262 fax 678-455-6264
www.marketplaceleaders.org
email: os@marketplaceleaders.org

Contents

Introduction 4

Lesson 1: The Fallacy of Full-Time Christian Work 7

Lesson 2: An Audience of One 10

Lesson 3: The Skillful Worker 13

Lesson 4: Understanding Our Own Calling 16

Lesson 5: Performing Miracles with Your Staff 19

Lesson 6: Your Work 22

Lesson 7: A Business Problem Leads to a Call 27

Lesson 8: Precious Deaths 31

Lesson 9: Stephen: A Marketplace Minister 35

Lesson 10: The Proper Foundation 38

Lesson 11: Living for a Greater Cause 41

Lesson 12: The Depth and Width of Your Calling 44

Introduction

I walked into the room and was greeted by a few men. They immediately identified themselves as recipients of *TGIF Today God Is First* marketplace meditations. They were grateful for the spiritual assistance it provided them in their journeys to apply biblical faith to their work life. However, their next comment surprised me. "We use your devotionals for our small group discussions before we begin our day." That prompted something inside.

Have you ever wandered into a Christian bookstore to try and find a Bible study resource related to the workplace? Chances are you will find that task rather difficult. I have realized over the years that this category—strangely where we spend over 70% of our time—has been overlooked by the mainstream body of Christ.

So, we decided to develop a small group study resource that uses the *TGIF Today God Is First* marketplace meditations as the central focal point. Each series of twelve studies will have a theme. The first theme in the series is on Calling.

How To Have An Effective Small Group Study

A friend of mine who is an orthodontist told me of a time when God led him to begin a Bible study on Monday mornings. He and his friend, another dentist, were to partner on the Bible study. Monday morning arrived and the two men were prepared to greet all those who had been invited to come. Ten minutes had gone by and no one had showed up. The dentist friend said, "Well, I guess we should just postpone until next week." My orthodontist friend replied, "Oh, no. It is time to begin. God told us to have this study. So, we must be good stewards and begin our study right now. My friend began to teach the Bible study to an empty room. Within the hour, men and women began to file into the room for the Monday morning gathering. By the end of the hour, several were in the room. Now, if my friends had decided to leave at that moment of doubt, they would have missed God for that day.

Many years ago, Oswald Chambers found himself in the same position when launching a Bible school. God told him to begin the school. The first day he had one student. But by the end of the first month, he was almost full.

Prayer: The First Step

Friend, the first thing you need to determine is whether God is leading you to begin a small group. Spend time seeking God's direction for such a gathering. Oswald Chambers said, "Much of Christian enterprise is Ishmael, seeking to do God's will in our own way—the one thing Jesus Christ never did." It is important to follow the guidance of the Holy Spirit in all we do. If we will do this, then we will birth something from the Spirit of God, not from our own effort. Once you have confirmation of direction, take the next step as He shows you.

Facilitator versus Teacher

Once you have a place and time selected, it is important to follow some basic principles in leading a small group.

Consider yourself a facilitator more than a teacher. This study guide is designed to provide the teaching necessary for the lesson. Your role is to create an atmosphere for learning and applying what is in the lesson. The lesson is designed to take up thirty to forty-five minutes of time. You can always expand with additional scriptures, questions, or comments from group members. You can also expand by having more time for prayer needs. Group participation is the key to having a successful group.

Open your time with prayer and ask God to lead your study. The Holy Spirit wants to lead your time. Let Him work. You will be amazed what God will do if you set the table for others to eat from.

After your time of study, have a few minutes for specific prayer for the members. This environment should be a safe place to share needs and get involved in the lives of the members of the group. The only reason you may not want to do this is if your group gets too large. However, if your group is less than ten or even fifteen, you should allow for this.

There are a few things you will want to stay away from when conducting a small group. If you are hosting a group with many different denominations represented, avoid negative comments about a particular denomination. Also, stay away from divisive topics that cannot be adequately addressed in a small group. There will be times when some questions arise that cannot be adequately addressed in the time you have together. Tell that person you will address their issue after your study time. Finally, you may have seekers join your group. We are all at different stages of our spiritual journeys. If you know you have unbelievers or new Christians in your group, stay away from religious language that these people may not be familiar with. Be sensitive to where people are.

We pray this study and future studies will be a blessing to you and those you serve. Let us know how we can improve these studies. Feel free to send us suggestions and comments.

God bless you. And remember, your work IS a ministry!

Os Hillman
Marketplace Leaders

TGIF Small Group Bible Study is published by Aslan Group Publishing.

Marketplace Leaders
3520 Habersham Club Drive
Cumming, Georgia 30041 USA
PHONE 678-455-6262 FAX 678-455-6264
www.marketplaceleaders.org
email: os@marketplaceleaders.org

The Fallacy of Full-Time Christian Work

Lesson 1

"I didn't know you were in full-time Christian work," said my close friend as we were driving. I responded, "Excuse me, but every person who has followed the will of God in their life is in full-time Christian work." God calls some to the mission field, others to be accountants, and others to be advertising executives, and still others to be construction workers.

God never made a distinction between sacred and secular. In fact, the Hebrew word *avodah* is the root word having the same meaning of "work" and "worship." God sees our work as worship.

We have incorrectly elevated the role of the Christian vocational worker to be more holy and committed than the person who is serving in a more secular environment. Yet, the call to the secular marketplace is as important as any other calling. God has to have His people in every sphere of life. Otherwise, many would never come to know Him.

I learned this lesson personally when I sought to go into "full-time" Christian service as a pastor in my late twenties, only to have God thrust me back into the business world unwillingly. This turned out to be the best thing He could have done for me because it was never His will for me to be a pastor. He knew I was more suited for the workplace.

We are all in missions. Some are called to foreign lands. Some are called to the jungles of the marketplace. Wherever you are called, serve the Lord in that place. Let Him demonstrate His power through your life so that others might experience Him through you today and see your vocation as worship to His glory.

WHATEVER YOU DO, WORK AT IT WITH ALL YOUR HEART, AS WORKING FOR THE LORD, NOT FOR MEN, SINCE YOU KNOW THAT YOU WILL RECEIVE AN INHERITANCE FROM THE LORD AS A REWARD. IT IS THE LORD CHRIST YOU ARE SERVING.

—COLOSSIANS 3:23-24

Discussion

What type of world would it be if every person in the world were a pastor or in vocational ministry?

How important is it to you that your dentist have training as a dentist? Why?

Why do you think God created human beings to have different interests and gifts? Was this just an afterthought from God?

How do you view your work?

In the beginning we do not train for God, we train for work, for our own aims; but as we go with God, we lose all our own aims and are trained into God's purpose. Unless practical work is appointed by God, it will prove a curse.
—OSWALD CHAMBERS

For Further Study

COLOSSIANS 3:17

COLOSSIANS 3:24

PSALM 90:17

1 CORINTHIANS 3:13

Workplace Application

God values our work even when the product has no eternal value. Christians often measure the significance of a job by its perceived value from the eternal perspective. Will the work last; will it "really count" for eternity? The implication is that God approves of work for eternity, but places little value on work for the here and now. By this measure, the work of ministers and missionaries has eternal value because it deals with people's spiritual, eternal needs. By contrast, the work of a salesman, bank teller, or typist has only limited value, because it meets only earthly needs. In other words, this kind of work doesn't really "count" in God's eyes. But this way of thinking overlooks several important truths.

> God himself has created a world that is time-bound and temporary. **2 PETER 3:10-11**
>
> Yet he values his work, declaring it to be "very good," by its very nature.
> **GENESIS 1:31; ACTS 14:17**
>
> God promises rewards to people in everyday jobs, based on their attitude and conduct.
> **EPHESIANS 6:8; COLOSSIANS 3:23-4:1**

God cares about the everyday needs of people as well as their spiritual needs. He cares whether people have food, clothing, and shelter.

"God cares about people who will enter eternity. To the extent that a job serves the needs of people, God values it, because he values people."[1]

Personal Reflection Notes

TGIF Action

"I am a servant of Jesus Christ, masquerading as a dentist," said my friend. This man had it right. He understood that his work life had an overriding ministry objective to it. This should be our attitude toward our work.

Today, begin seeing your work as a calling from God.

ROMANS 11:28-30

...for God's gifts and his call are irrevocable.

Lesson 2

Do not conform any longer to the pattern of this world, but be transformed by the renewing of your mind. Then you will be able to test and approve what God's will is—His good, pleasing and perfect will.
—Romans 12:2

An Audience of One

What audience do you play to? Each day you are seen by many who will make a judgment about the way you handle yourself among different audiences. Politicians have learned to play to their audiences, customizing messages for the needs of their particular groups. Musicians have learned to play to their audiences. Pastors play to their congregations each Sunday morning. Businesspeople play to the audiences who will buy their product.

Christ has called us to play to one audience—the audience of Himself. When you seek to please any other audience in your life, you become susceptible to situational ethics and motivations based on the need for the moment. Your audience becomes a pawn in your hands because you know what they want. Is that wrong? Sometimes it is, sometimes it isn't.

Pure obedience to pleasing God in our lives will often meet the needs of those around us. It is God's will that you and I love our spouses, provide good services to our customers, and look to the interests of others before ourselves. This will result in meeting many needs of the audiences in our lives.

However, there are other times when our audiences may ask for something contrary to God's will. Politicians are often forced to appease their audiences, even though it may go against God's laws. When we are asked to go with the flow, we discover which audience is most important in our lives. Is it the audience of One, or the audience of many?

Who are the audiences in your life?
What are the dangers of playing exclusively to the needs of an audience?

How do you know when you are playing to an audience instead of playing to the "audience of one?"

What steps could you take that would protect you from making choices purely on the perception of what others will think?

Discussion

It is nonsense to imagine that God expects me to discern all that is clear to His own mind; all He asks of me is maintain perfect confidence in Him. Faith springs from the indwelling of the life of God in me.
—OSWALD CHAMBERS

For Further Study

JOHN 21:20-23

1 CORINTHIANS 3:5-15

1 CORINTHIANS 3:18-23

1 CORINTHIANS 4:1-5

TGIF Action

Today, be aware of which audience you are playing to. *Ask yourself why you are taking a particular action.* Is it to please the audience of One? Or is it to please the audience of others who might negatively impact you should you not play to their tune?

Workplace Application

Jesus gave them this answer:

> *"I tell you the truth, the Son can do nothing by himself; he can do only what he sees his Father doing, because whatever the Father does the Son also does. For the Father loves the Son and shows him all he does. Yes, to your amazement he will show him even greater things than these."*
>
> **JOHN 5:19-20**

Christ was not driven by public opinion. He only did what the Father told him to do. Jesus represented a life lived to please an audience of One. We live in a day when we are often driven by the latest opinion poll. There is only one decision to be made—the right one. No matter the cost.

God calls you and I into an intimacy with Himself. That intimacy with God allows us to hear his voice, and to be led by the Holy Spirit. If you are to fulfill your workplace calling, you must do so by living to an audience of One.

Personal Reflection Notes

The Skillful Worker

Lesson 3

The Lord has called each of us to be excellent in what we do. Those whom God used in the Kingdom as marketplace ministers were skilled and exemplified excellence in their field. Not only were these men skilled, they were filled with God's Spirit.

Then the Lord said to Moses,

> *"See, I have chosen Bezalel son of Uri, the son of Hur, of the tribe of Judah, and I have filled him with the Spirit of God, with skill, ability and knowledge in all kinds of crafts—to make artistic designs for work in gold, silver and bronze, to cut and set stones, to work in wood, and to engage in all kinds of craftsmanship."* **Exodus 31:1-5**

Consider Huram, a craftsman of bronze in whom Solomon entrusted much of the temple designs. God's word says he was a true master craftsman (see 1 Kings 7:14). Consider Joseph, whose skill as an administrator was known throughout Egypt and the world. Consider Daniel, who served his king with great skill and integrity. The list goes on and on—David, Nehemiah, Acquilla and Priscilla, to name a few.

I recall the first issue of an international publication that we began. It was common to hear the comment, "It doesn't even look like a Christian magazine." They were saying the quality and excellence exceeded what they equated to Christian work. What a shame. Has inferior quality become synonymous with Christian work?

May we strive for excellence in all that we do for the Master of the universe.

> *"Whatever you do, work at it with all your heart, as working for the Lord, not for men, since you know that you will receive an inheritance from the Lord as a reward."* **Colossians 3:23-24**

Do you see a man skilled in his work? He will serve before kings; he will not serve before obscure men.
—**Proverbs 22:29**

It is the Lord Christ you are serving.

Discussion

God comes into our mortal flesh and we do our ordinary work, in an ordinary setting, among ordinary people, as we would do it for Him.
—**Oswald Chambers**

The Exodus 31 passage says that Bezalel was chosen by God and was filled with the Spirit of God to design the ark of the covenant and other instruments to go inside the ark. What does this say about how we should view our work?

Bezalel is one of the first persons in the Bible that is described as one who is filled with the Spirit of God. It is significant to note this person was a craftsman and not a priest. Scholars tell us whenever things are first mentioned in the Bible we should take note. What does this say about the importance of being filled with the Spirit of God and skillful in our work?

Bezalel was called to design and build the place where the presence of God would dwell. You and I are called to create a workplace where God can dwell. If this is the case, what things might you do that will create a workplace environment where the presence of God might dwell? Give some examples of things you can do to create such an environment.

Workplace Application

Have you ever felt that your "secular" work was less than spiritual? Do you think Bezalel felt that way? Sure, he worked on a "spiritual" project. But he did not always do this. God prepared him for many years for this ultimate task. You must not consider your secular work as unspiritual or something that does not contribute to the kingdom of God.

We are all called to perform our daily tasks as unto the Lord (Colossians 3:17). Be aware that as you seek to be the best at what you do for the glory of God, He will bring glory to Himself in ways you may not be able to see right now.

Personal Reflection Notes

TGIF Action

Today, realize God has given you the skill and ability to do what you are doing. You may not "feel" that what you are doing is very spiritual. However, realize that it is not the activity as much as the motive and attitude that God will use to bring glory to Himself through what you are doing.

Ask God to fill you with His Holy Spirit so that you will be found worthy of the calling He has placed upon your life.

For Further Study

John 17:4

Philippians 1:12

Jeremiah 29:11

Romans 9:5

Lesson 4

Understanding Our Own Calling

...If I want him to remain alive until I return, what is that to you? You must follow Me.
—John 21:22

We need to be about godly ambition in order to see our works as "God-works."

Jesus was talking to Peter after he had just had a very important encounter with Him—one of the last meetings the two would have. This was the third time Jesus had shown Himself to the disciples after His resurrection. It is the famous dialogue between Jesus and Peter in which Jesus asked Peter three times if he loved Him. Jesus followed by commanding, "Feed My sheep." Jesus went on to foretell of Peter's future death. As they were walking together, Peter noticed that John was following them. Peter immediately asked Jesus what His plans were for John. Jesus reacted sharply to Peter's question, telling him not to worry about what John's role or purpose was in life. All Peter had to do was worry about fulfilling his own purpose.

As marketplace Christians we tend to measure our success on whether we have achieved a certain position or stature in life. Even as believers the temptation to think that someone is blessed if they have achieved prominence is always confronting us. In His discussion with Peter, Jesus was getting at the very heart of the matter of a person's calling. Peter was worried about whether his friend John was going to get the same lot in life as he was. Jesus told him it should not be his concern. He was to concern himself only with one thing: his own calling before God.

To this John replied, "A man can receive only what is given him from heaven. You yourselves can testify that I said, `I am not the Christ but am sent ahead of him.'" **John 3:27-29**

Discussion

Ambition can become a danger to the purposes of God in our lives. If the ambition and motive is not centered in obedience to Jesus Christ, we can easily fall prey to envy. What happens when we begin to envy the position or place of another?

We only have to remain true to God, and when His word is fulfilled, we know it because it will be supernatural fulfillment. We must learn the difference between helping God and God helping us.
—OSWALD CHAMBERS

How would you define envy as compared to contentment? Read 1 Timothy 6:16. Describe the balance between godly ambition and godly contentment. What should be our motive for success?

Read Ephesians 2:10. Do you know the good works God has prepared for you to do? Are you doing it?

For Further Study

PROVERBS 16:2

1 CORINTHIANS 4:5

JAMES 4:3

PSALM 127:1

TGIF Action

Are you tempted to compare yourself with where others are in their life? Are you dissatisfied with where God has you right now?

Be of good cheer: "[be] confident of this, that He who began a good work in you will carry it on to completion until the day of Christ Jesus."
–PHILIPPIANS 1:6

If you find yourself envying the life of another person, repent before the Lord and ask God to fulfill His purposes in your life.

Workplace Application

Sometimes our ambition is motivated from fear of failure or the desire to gain wealth or position. John the Baptist understood what he was to receive and what he was not to receive (see John 3:27). A mature believer understands how to move in his/her workplace calling by realizing what God has called them to. Sometimes we sweat and toil to receive things God never intended for us to have. We need to be about godly ambition in order to see our works as God-works, not just good-works. Is there any activity in your life that is merely a good-work, versus a God-work?

Personal Reflection Notes

Performing Miracles with Your Staff

Lesson 5

Moses' staff represented his vocation as a shepherd. God had something in mind for his vocation—to perform miracles. And what awesome miracles He did! God turned the Nile river into blood with the touch of Moses' staff. He turned the staff into a snake. He parted the Red Sea with it. These are just a few of the miracles God did with Moses' staff. What is the staff God has put into your hand? Is it being a builder? Is it being an office worker? Is it being a doctor?

When we yield our talents and abilities to the Lord, God can perform miracles through them. First, Moses had to yield what He had in his hand to God. He had to lay it down. God transformed his staff into a snake. Moses had never seen his staff in this way. God also told him to pick it up by the tail, something we are cautioned never to do. Only after Moses viewed his staff in a different light could God use that staff. As long as Moses held onto it, God could not and would not perform miracles through it.

Until we come to this place with our heavenly Father, we will fail to see miracles performed in our work. He delights in showing His power through us. When we become an open vessel, we can expect to see things happen.

> *And whatever you do, whether in word or deed, do it all in the name of the Lord Jesus, giving thanks to God the Father through him.* **COLOSSIANS 3:17**

BUT TAKE THIS STAFF IN YOUR HAND SO YOU CAN PERFORM MIRACULOUS SIGNS WITH IT.

—EXODUS 4:17

God wants to change your paradigm about your view of your work.

Discussion

God's omniscience, God's order, and God's opportunity all work together in an individual's life, and Jesus Christ enters into our lives right into the midst of seemingly haphazard circumstances.
—OSWALD CHAMBERS

When is the last time something happened in your workplace that could only be explained as "God?" Describe.

If you cannot cite an example it may mean you are not experiencing the power of God in your workplace calling. God wants to reveal Himself in your workplace. What is required of us in order for God to use our "staff" to perform miracles?

What does the following scripture say about the attitude of Paul regarding the evidence of God in his life?

> *My message and my preaching were not with wise and persuasive words, but with a demonstration of the Spirit's power, so that your faith might not rest on men's wisdom, but on God's power.*
>
> 1 CORINTHIANS 2:4-5

For Further Study

JOEL 3:10

ACTS 6:1-7

EPHESIANS 1:18-19

MARK 11:22-24

Workplace Application

The Lord wants to demonstrate His power in your workplace in order that others might know that the power of God is real and personal. When I led a man to Christ at a company that I was consulting with, I was able to see the power of God working in my workplace. When God met an unexpected financial need that could only be explained as God, others began to ask about my faith. When I prayed that God would "move the mountain" of inventoried books in my basement and a large order came three hours later, God demonstrated His power in my work.

Consult with God about every detail of your daily responsibilities in your workplace. Then, you will see God manifest His power through your life in your workplace calling.

Personal Reflection Notes

TGIF Action

Have you given your "staff" to the Lord? Offer it to Him and see what He might want to do through it. Your life will never be the same.

Giving our "staff" to the Lord is the first step.

Lesson 6

I HAVE BROUGHT YOU GLORY ON EARTH BY COMPLETING THE WORK YOU GAVE ME TO DO.

—JOHN 17:4

YOUR WORK

The Lord has revealed to us that the number one thing we are to do is love the Lord our God with all our heart and to love our neighbor as ourselves. His desire is for us to know Him and the power of His resurrection. These mandates deal with our relationship with Him. The fruit of this relationship must then result in our glorifying Him by completing the work He has given each of us to do. It will become a by-product of this relationship, not an end in itself.

What is the work God has called you to do? Jesus never did anything the Father had not instructed Him to do. He lived in such communion with the Father that He knew when to turn to the left and when to turn to the right. Is it possible to have such a relationship with our heavenly Father? I think that if it weren't, He would not have given us such an example.

> *Call to Me and I will answer you and tell you great and unsearchable things you do not know.*
>
> **JEREMIAH 33:3**

What has He called you to do? Perhaps you are called to be the best CPA in your city or the best advertising executive or the best office worker or assembly-line person in your company. Whatever work He has called you to do, He will use you as His instrument to accomplish something that He has uniquely prepared you to do. Men and women in the workplace tend to be task-oriented. They want to get things done. However, there is a danger in being action-oriented when we seek to accomplish things outside the power of God. Read the following passages and discuss their implications.

> *I want to know Christ and the power of his resurrection and the fellowship of sharing in his sufferings, becoming like him in his death, and so, somehow, to attain to the resurrection from the dead.*
>
> **PHILIPPIANS 3:10-11**

Discussion

Paul was a "get-things-done" kind of guy. Yet, we discover that there was something even more important than what he did for God. What was that and why do you think Paul felt this was so important?

So often we focus on the "doing" versus the "being" in our calling before God. However, God wants us to know Him intimately, and to know His love for us. The passage to the right describes Paul's prayer that we come to know Christ and His love personally. More than anything else, God wants us to comprehend the deep love He has for each of us. What is the relationship between our knowing the love of God, and the works God will do through us based on this knowledge?

What is the danger of doing works that are not founded in His love?

I pray that out of his glorious riches he may strengthen you with power through his Spirit in your inner being, so that Christ may dwell in your hearts through faith. And I pray that you, being rooted and established in love, may have power, together with all the saints, to grasp how wide and long and high and deep is the love of Christ, and to know this love that surpasses knowledge—that you may be filled to the measure of all the fullness of God. Now to him who is able to do immeasurably more than all we ask or imagine, according to his power that is at work within us, to him be glory in the church and in Christ Jesus throughout all generations, for ever and ever! Amen.

—EPHESIANS 3:16-21

What has He called you to do?

Much of modern Christian enterprise is "Ishmael." Born not of God, but of an inordinate desire to do God's will in our own way—the one thing our Lord never did.
—**OSWALD CHAMBERS**

For Further Study

PSALM 147:10-11

ISAIAH 31:1

DEUTERONOMY 8:17-9:1

Workplace Application

> *Unless the LORD builds the house, its builders labor in vain. Unless the LORD watches over the city, the watchmen stand guard in vain. In vain you rise early and stay up late, toiling for food to eat—for he grants sleep to those he loves.*
>
> **PSALMS 127:1-2**

George Washington Carver lived in the early 1900s. He was credited with more than 300 inventions for marketable products related to the peanut, and more than 100 for the sweet potato. His discoveries transformed the southern economy. Early in the morning Carver would go to his lab and ask God, "Lord, why did you make the peanut?" During those times, God would give him insight into the peanut and sweet potato. He credits His time with God early in the morning as the source of his inspiration and discoveries.

Henry Blackaby, author of *Experiencing God*, challenged some Fortune 500 CEOs to spend time with God in the early morning. At first, they challenged him, explaining that they were much too busy. However, one man took his advice. Here is what he discovered.

> *"I took you seriously, and I'm getting up at 4 o'clock in the morning. It's been the greatest time-saver I've ever known. Because what God says to me in the early hours shapes the direction of my day; I know what to do and what not to do. I didn't realize that that meeting with God was the greatest time-saver. I led my first employee to the Lord because God gave me direction, I obeyed, and I began to see Him at work."* —*Religion Today*, March 7, 2001

Your key to having a successful walk with God that bears fruit in your spiritual and professional life is dependent upon how well you know and follow God. Make a priority to spend time with God and you will discover new strategies to succeed in your life and work.

Personal Reflection Notes

TGIF Action

When our life is complete, what a glorious day it will be if we can each say, "I have completed the work You gave me to do." This will have brought great glory to Him.

Today, before you begin your day, ask God what He would have you accomplish this day. Pray that He might accomplish the tasks He wants to accomplish through you.

The direction of duty lies not in doing things for God, but in doing what God tell us to do.

—OSWALD CHAMBERS

Lesson 7

A Business Problem Leads to a Call

NOW THE DONKEYS BELONGING TO SAUL'S FATHER KISH WERE LOST, AND KISH SAID TO HIS SON SAUL, "TAKE ONE OF THE SERVANTS WITH YOU AND GO AND LOOK FOR THE DONKEYS."

—1 SAMUEL 9:3

The people of Israel wanted a king. God finally agreed. Samuel was the prophet of Israel who was to anoint the man God had chosen. God selected a young man to be the first king of Israel—his name was Saul.

It is interesting to look at the circumstances in which God called Saul into his new vocation. It seems that Saul's father had a business that used donkeys. During those times, donkeys were often used for commerce. It was obviously important to Saul's father to find the lost donkeys, so he sent Saul and his servant out to find them.

They went from region to region, unable to find the donkeys. Finally, Saul told his servant that they should go back. He thought that his father would be worried. But the servant replied,

> *"Look, in this town there is a man of God; he is highly respected, and everything he says comes true. Let's go there now. Perhaps he will tell us what way to take."* **1 SAMUEL 9:6**

Saul took his advice. Near the town they met some young girls who told them that Samuel had just come to their town that day. When they arrived, they met Samuel who told them that the donkeys were safe and he would also tell Saul the next morning all that was in his heart. He then informed Saul of his new calling to be the next king of Israel.

God brought a workplace problem into Saul's life so that he would discover God's call in his life.

Saul and his servant spent three days hunting for their lost donkeys. What correlation do you see in their actions and the actions of most people when it comes to solving problems?

> *"I am the seer," Samuel replied. "Go up ahead of me to the high place, for today you are to eat with me, and in the morning I will let you go and will tell you all that is in your heart. As for the donkeys you lost three days ago, do not worry about them; they have been found. And to whom is all the desire of Israel turned, if not to you and all your father's family?"*
> **1 SAMUEL 9:19-20**

When Samuel greeted Saul and his servant, he let him know immediately the situation. What did Samuel say about the problem they were seeking to solve? What does this say about our problems?

God has already solved your problem. His solution may not have been revealed to you yet. He is waiting for you and I to become part of the solution. Many times God does not solve a problem until we are willing to comply with His will regarding the situation. What is the first thing we should do when we encounter a problem?

Discussion

God often creates a crisis in our lives to lead us into a new calling.

For Further Study

1 THESSALONIANS 5:4

JEREMIAH 9:23

JOHN 10:3

TGIF Action

Can you see what circumstances led to Saul's receiving his call? It started with a business problem—lost donkeys. It led to connecting Saul with Samuel through a number of divine appointments and circumstances. God still does this today.

God will provide the necessary circumstances to accomplish His purposes in your life. You must realize that a workplace problem may lead to a new calling for your life. Saul had no idea lost donkeys would be the instrument used to change his life. So, too, we must realize God's ways are not our ways.

Workplace Application

One time I was a speaker at a Christian business conference in Singapore. The night before I was to speak, I was prompted by the Holy Spirit to modify my presentation to include the passage below and its application to men and women in the workplace. The following morning my wife and I had breakfast with Maggie, one of the intercessors for the conference. She had prepared for the conference by fasting and praying forty days for this event. I asked Maggie, "Has the Lord spoken to you about this conference as you have been praying for it?" She smiled and said excitedly, "Oh, yes! The Lord said the business people of Singapore were to give their 'donkeys' (businesses) to the Lord." That day was the day men and women in the Singapore business community stepped forward and gave their "donkeys" to the Lord.

Have you given your work to the Lord?

> *"As they approached Jerusalem and came to Bethphage on the Mount of Olives, Jesus sent two disciples, saying to them, 'Go to the village ahead of you, and at once you will find a donkey tied there, with her colt by her. Untie them and bring them to me. If anyone says anything to you, tell him that the Lord needs them, and he will send them right away.'"* **MATTHEW 21:1-3**

Personal Reflection Notes

PRECIOUS DEATHS

Lesson 8

PRECIOUS IN THE SIGHT OF THE LORD IS THE DEATH OF HIS SAINTS.
—PSALM 116:15

The Bible often speaks of death as a requirement of living a life in Christ. This death is not a physical death, but a spiritual death. It is a death of the old so the new can be raised. It is the life of Christ that is raised in us. However, this death can be painful if we do not choose to willingly allow this "circumcision of heart" to have its way. If we are not circumcised of heart, we do not enter into God's promises. Moses was called to deliver a people from slavery. But when he was about to return to Egypt to begin what God called Him to do, God almost killed him. He had failed to take care of the details of obedience. In this case, it was that all the males in his family were to be circumcised. This oversight on Moses' part almost cost him his life. Imagine that—God prepared a man 40 years, and yet, he was almost disqualified because of an oversight.

> *"At a lodging place on the way, the Lord met Moses and was about to kill him. But Zipporah took a flint knife, cut off her son's foreskin and touched Moses' feet with it...."* **EXODUS 4:24**

None of us will ever enter the Promised Land of full blessing with God unless we have this same circumcision of heart. The psalmist above accurately describes the process of circumcising the heart.

> *Precious in the sight of the Lord is the death of His saints. O Lord, truly I am Your servant; I am Your servant, the son of Your maidservant; You have freed me from my chains.* **PSALM 116:15-16**

We cannot be free to be God's servant until this death takes place in each of us. When this death takes place, we become free—free from the chains of sin that held us back from becoming completely His. Oh, what freedom there is when this death takes place. No longer are we held to the sin of materialism, fear, self-effort, or anxiety; for we are dead to these things.

The Bible speaks of the seed that must die in order for it to spring up and give new life.

> *I tell you the truth, unless a kernel of wheat falls to the ground and dies, it remains only a single seed. But if it dies, it produces many seeds. The man who loves his life will lose it, while the man who hates his life in this world will keep it for eternal life.*
>
> **JOHN 12:24-25**

Discussion

Why do you think God requires a "circumcision of heart"? Describe what you think this process looks like for the believer. How does one know if they have had a circumcision of heart?

When you obey the call of God, the first thing that strikes you is the irrelevancy of the thing you have to do.
—OSWALD CHAMBERS

> *The man who loves his life will lose it, while the man who hates his life in this world will keep it for eternal life. Whoever serves me must follow me; and where I am, my servant also will be. My Father will honor the one who serves me.* **JOHN 12:25-26**

What might a person's life look like who "hates his life in this world"? How might the Father honor the one who serves Him?

Read and discuss the following passage that may shed some light on the previous question.

> *But the fruit of the Spirit is love, joy, peace, patience, kindness, goodness, faithfulness, gentleness and self-control. Against such things there is no law. Those who belong to Christ Jesus have crucified the sinful nature with its passions and desires. Since we live by the Spirit, let us keep in step with the Spirit. Let us not become conceited, provoking and envying each other.* GALATIANS 5:22-26

Discuss some attributes of a person who is walking "in the Spirit."

Workplace Application

For years I lived a Christian life that did all the right things. However, there were areas that I consciously and unconsciously had not given over to the lordship of Christ. The Lord brought a crisis in my life to allow me to see I had not given over these areas to Him. Sometimes God allows circumstances to develop so that we may see the areas of our lives that have not yet been yielded to Him. It could be a situation in your office that reveals anger. We could get overlooked for a promotion that yields striving. He may allow many different situations to reveal what is in our heart. Yielding your life to the purposes of God is a daily experience.

TGIF Action

Each of us must ask the Lord if our seed has "died." Is it in the ground now, yielding the fruit of brokenness before Him? This is the great paradox of a life in Christ—-the circumcision of heart and the death process.

Ask God to free you to become all that He wants you to be today. Then you will begin to walk in new freedom and see God begin to multiply your seed to others. You will begin to see God work in your workplace and your life like never before.

Personal Reflection Notes

For Further Study

ROMANS 8:12-15

ROMANS 6:4

ROMANS 6:11-14

JEREMIAH 9:23-25

Stephen: A Marketplace Minister

Lesson 9

In the beginning of the early church, the disciples were seeing God move in mighty ways. The disciples found themselves preaching the word of God all over the region. However, there became practical needs that arose among the people, but due to their preaching these needs were not being met adequately. One of these needs involved food distribution to widows. This brought pressure upon the disciples who felt their primary focus must be to preach the gospel. They realized they could not do both adequately which led them to appoint seven men whose lives qualified for service as leaders to meet these needs.

This is a remarkable turning point in the early church. When this action took place, we see a number of things happen. The first man named to fill this responsibility was Stephen, described as a man full of faith and the Holy Ghost; with a strong faith in Christ. He was full of courage, gifts and graces. He was an extraordinary man, and excelled in every thing that was good; his name signified a crown.

We also see in this passage an empowering of the rest of the marketplace believers into service. But it is important to see that Stephen was more than just a person who could lend a hand to the service needs of the local church. The Bible describes Stephen this way:

> *Now Stephen, a man full of God's grace and power, did great wonders and miraculous signs among the people.* **Acts 6:8-9**

This was a time when the church began mobilizing other marketplace believers for ministry in the community. Stephen was the first chosen and interestingly, became the first martyred believer. One of the most interesting things one can notice when the disciples took this action is described in these passages. *"So the*

These men began to argue with Stephen, but they could not stand up against his wisdom or the Spirit by whom he spoke.
– Acts 6:9-10

word of God spread. The number of disciples in Jerusalem increased rapidly, and a large number of priests became obedient to the faith" (Acts 6:7). It is as though the Lord took the cap off and everything started happening. Even a large number of priests came into the faith.

*The church often trains us to do **their** ministry instead of **our** ministry.*
—**Dr. Myles Munroe**

Today, we live in a time of paradigm shifting in the body of Christ. God is beginning a movement among those in the workplace. You and I are part of this movement. As more and more men and women take their rightful place as workplace ministers with signs and wonders that accompany their life, we will begin to see pastors and church leaders understand this movement and begin to embrace it. It will be the fruit of the lives of these marketplace ministers and the power of God that changes the old paradigms. However, be sure of this, whenever there is a move of God, there is also opposition by Satan that comes from the religious leadership, just as it did in the early church movement.

Discussion

Stephen, like most of the disciples, probably had an occupation that earned him a living. Yet, we find Stephen had a reputation as a godly man. Describe the qualities of Stephen as listed in Acts 6 verses 5 and 8.

When the disciples added seven new disciples to help with the load, what was the direct result of their actions? Why do you think it was important to lay hands on them and pray for them? See Acts 6:7.

For Further Study

1 Corinthians 16:19

Romans 16:3

Acts 1:8

Why do you think priests became obedient to the faith? Why do you think persecution also came from the religious community?

TGIF Action

Do you view yourself less spiritual than someone else? Do you ever think that spiritual matters should be left to the "clergy"?

There is no biblical basis for this belief. God wants you and I to experience His power and presence in our daily work life.

Take an inventory of your life today and determine if someone could describe your life as a person "full of faith and of the Holy Spirit, full of grace and power, and one who does great wonders and miraculous things." If they can't, begin asking God today to accomplish this in your life.

Workplace Application

When I began writing the *TGIF Today God Is First* devotionals I received many letters from readers around the world. One time I received a short note from a pastor who asked, "How does a businessman have such wisdom?" This statement spoke volumes to me about the misconception that so many, especially pastors, have about men and women in the workplace. The underlying message is, "I have greater spiritual insights because I am in vocational ministry." It also revealed his experience. He had not known someone in the workplace to have deep spiritual insight. Whether we work in "vocational ministry" or "secular ministry", we must realize God is no respecter of persons when it comes to following Him. Obedience, motivated out of love for Jesus, will determine the level of spiritual maturity of the believer. It has little to do with our vocational status. God has called each of us to walk with Him in our daily lives.

Personal Reflection Notes

THE PROPER FOUNDATION

Lesson 10

Imagine spending years building an expensive home with the finest materials and craftsmanship. It is a work of art, and the project is almost complete. As the day arrives to move in, a building inspector comes and hands you a notice condemning your beautiful home because it doesn't meet code.

Many Christians in the workplace invest years in their vocations will one day stand before the Lord and realize *they* were building the house, not the *Lord*. God is very picky about the motives behind our actions. Before we act, we must ask why. *Why* are we doing what we are doing? Has God called us to this task? Or is the real motive purely financial? Or control? Or prestige?

> *If any man builds on this foundation using gold, silver, costly stones, wood, hay or straw, his work will be shown for what it is, because the Day will bring it to light. It will be revealed with fire, and the fire will test the quality of each man's work.*
>
> **1 CORINTHIANS 3:12-13**

David learned this principle by the end of his life. Throughout his life he had learned that God always tested him to find out what was in his heart, and what his motive was behind his actions. David instructed his son to "...acknowledge the God of your father, and serve Him with wholehearted devotion and with a willing mind, for the Lord searches every heart and understands every motive behind the thoughts" (1 Chronicles 28:9a).

Paul said what had happened to him had served to advance the gospel. Have the adversities in your life and the blessings in your life advanced the gospel?

UNLESS THE LORD BUILDS THE HOUSE, ITS BUILDERS LABOR IN VAIN.
– PSALM 127:1A

Discussion

What happens to a building that has a poor foundation?

What happens when we work with only the motive of making money?

What does it mean to seek God's hand versus His face?

The depth and width of your faith experiences are directly proportional to the calling upon your life.

For Further Study

John 6:26

Proverbs 16:2

1 Chronicles 28:9

1 Corinthians 4:5

Workplace Application

When I began writing *TGIF*, I knew my motive was to provide a helpful tool for others. I was developing content based on the word of God (foundation and motive). God confirmed my writing through many others who would let me know how much it was helping them (confirmation). However, I was not trained to be a writer. It had been years since I had been in an English grammar class. God brought editors into my life to help me become more *skillful* in my calling.

Personal Reflection Notes

TGIF Action

There are four things to consider before you begin any enterprise.

First, make sure your foundation is based on Jesus Christ. Seek His will on the matter.

Second, look for confirmation of your decision. God wants to reveal His will through His word, circumstances, relationships and the Holy Spirit.

Third, ask *why* you want to do this. What is your real motive?

Finally, do you have the skill and ability to accomplish the task? Some things require more training than others.

Consider what skills you need to excel in the venture.

Lesson 11

LIVING FOR A GREATER CAUSE

I CAN DO EVERYTHING THROUGH HIM WHO GIVES ME STRENGTH.
– PHILIPPIANS 4:13

"Hello, my name is Dr. Glover, a servant of Jesus Christ, masquerading as a dentist."

What does it mean for workplace believers to live for a cause greater than themselves in our day and time? Jeremiah Lanphier was a businessman in New York City who asked God to do this in his life in 1857.

In a small darkened room, in the back of one of New York City's lesser churches, he prayed alone. His request of God was simple, but earth-shattering: *"Lord, what wilt Thou have me to do?"*

He was a man approaching midlife without a wife or family, but he had financial means. He made a decision to reject the "success syndrome" that drove the city's businessmen and bankers. God used him to turn New York City's commercial empire on its head. He began a businessmen's prayer meeting on September 23, 1857. The meetings began slowly, but six months later, 30,000 were meeting daily throughout the city. The *New York Tribune* and the *New York Herald* issued articles of revival. It had become the city's biggest news. Now a full-fledged revival, it moved outside New York. By spring of 1858, 2,000 met daily in Chicago's Metropolitan Theatre, and in Philadelphia the meetings mushroomed into a four-month long tent meeting. Meetings were held in Baltimore, Washington, Cincinnati, Chicago, New Orleans, and Mobile. Thousands met to pray because one man stepped out. *Annus Mirabilis*, the year of national revival, had begun.[2]

This was an extraordinary move of God through one man. It was unique because the movement was led by businessmen, a group long considered the least prone to any form of evangelical fervor, and it had started on Wall Street, the most unlikely of all places to begin.

Could God do something extraordinary through you? Take a step. Ask God to do mighty things through you.

Discussion

Jeremiah Lanphier was a catalyst to bring revival to a nation in 1857. What qualities do you think this man must have had to be used of God in this way?

Fear of failure prevents many people from stepping out in faith to be used by God. What is required to move beyond a fear of failure?

When Jeremiah Lanphier first began to meet for prayer at the noon hour, he had very few people show up. What would have been the consequence if he had called it quits after 30-days?

We must make decisions based on obedience, not outcome. God never called on you to make an outcome-based decision.

For Further Study

MATTHEW 19:26

MARK 11:22-24

HEBREWS 11:1-2

JUDGES 6:11-12

TGIF Action

Have you ever thought about starting a Bible study or prayer group at your workplace but were afraid no one might show up?

Fear of failure prevents many people from being used by God. If God prompts you to do something, step out in obedience. He is bigger than our weaknesses or mistakes. He will honor your motive to serve others. He wants to reveal Himself through your act of obedience.

Workplace Application

Two businessmen believed God wanted them to start a Bible study at their office on Monday mornings. Monday morning arrived and they were prepared to begin the study. There was only one problem—there were no people in the room. No one had shown up. "I guess we should try next week," said one of the men. "Oh, no," said the other, "God told us to begin this study." The man stood up and began to teach the Bible study to an empty room out of obedience. Soon, people began to file into the room. By the end of the hour, several people had shown up for the study.

Personal Reflection Notes

The Depth and Width of Your Calling

Lesson 12

"God must love you a lot! He doesn't allow someone to go through the kinds of adversity you have experienced unless He has a special calling on your life." Those were the words spoken to me by two different mentors at two different times within a three-year period. Later I would learn another related truth from a respected man of God—a man whom God uses throughout the globe. "The depth and width of your faith experiences are directly proportional to your calling." What were these men of God saying?

They were describing a process of preparation that God takes each of His leaders through when He plans to use them in significant ways. A "faith experience" is an event or "spiritual marker" in your life about which you can say, "That is where I saw God personally move in my life." God showed Himself personally to you in an unmistakable event. It was the burning bush for Moses; the Jordan River for the nation of Israel; or Jacob's encounter with the angel. It was the feeding of the 5,000 for the disciples. It was the time when you saw God face to face in your life.

If God has plans of using you in the lives of many others, you can expect that He is going to allow certain faith experiences to come into your life in order to build a foundation that will be solid. That foundation is what you will be able to look back on to keep you faithful to Him in the times of testing. Each of us must have personal faith experiences in which we experience God personally so that we can move in faith to whatever He may call us. Do you need a personal faith experience right now in your life? Pray that God will reveal Himself to you. He delights in doing that.

IF WE ARE DISTRESSED, IT IS FOR YOUR COMFORT AND SALVATION; IF WE ARE COMFORTED, IT IS FOR YOUR COMFORT, WHICH PRODUCES IN YOU PATIENT ENDURANCE OF THE SAME SUFFERINGS WE SUFFER.

–2 Corinthians 1:6

Discussion

The more we have to sacrifice for God, the more glorious the reward. We have no right to choose our sacrifice; however, God will let us see what our 'Israel' is to be."

—OSWALD CHAMBERS

Describe a faith experience event in your life in which you experienced God in a very personal way.

If the depth and width of our faith experiences often determine the level of call upon our lives, how should we view difficult trials that may come into our lives?

For Further Study

GENESIS 14:10-22
JOSHUA 3:14-17
JOSHUA 6

Why are "faith experiences" important for the Christian?

Workplace Application

It was March of 1998. God had miraculously provided the money for me to attend a Christian business conference on the island of Cyprus. After I led a morning devotional time, a man from England came up to me. "I need to talk to you," he said. I did not share any of my personal life in the message that morning, so he knew nothing of my series of financial crises that were part of my life at the time. He said, "The Lord wants you to know He had to remove your finances to insure the reward He has for you in Heaven." I was shocked! How could this man know my situation? A few moments later, we were praying together. While in prayer he said, "I see a tree. It is full of fruit and the fruit is now beginning to fall. You are the tree." I began to weep. That was the third prayer incident over the last three years in which someone had described my life as a tree—however, this was the first time the fruit was falling.

God allowed me to have this "faith experience" to encourage me in my faith journey. He wants to do the same for you.

Personal Reflection Notes

TGIF Action

Has God ever taken you to your own "Red Sea" experience where if you did not receive a breakthrough, you might be overcome by the circumstance?

God often sets up situations in order to frame your life through the experience.
God wants to build a testimony through your life. Begin to look for opportunities to experience the power of Christ in your circumstances.

Marketplace Leaders/Aslan Group Publishing
3520 Habersham Club Drive
Cumming, Georgia 30041 USA
678-455-6262 fax 678-455-6264
www.marketplaceleaders.org
email: os@marketplaceleaders.org

[1] *Word in Life Study Bible* notes, p.1869, Thomas Nelson Publishers, Nashville, 1993.

[2] John Woodbridge, ed., *More Than Conquerors* (Chicago, Illinois: Moody Press, 1992), 337.

All quotes by Oswald Chambers, used with permission. *Not Knowing Where,* Oswald Chambers, Discovery House Publishing.

Other Resources by Os Hillman

TGIF Today God Is First

365 Meditations on the Principles of Christ in the Workplace.

It began as a series of daily e-mail meditations for his business associates. Today, it is one of the fastest growing devotionals on the internet and is now a book of 365 daily meditations especially geared for men and women in the workplace. Os has the uncanny ability to write just to people's circumstances to help men and women understand how to walk with God in the everyday trials of life. *hardback*

The Purposes of Money

Exposing the Five Fallacies About Money and God's Five Purposes for Its Use

One day a series of crises entered the world of this successful advertising agency executive that would alter his life forever. These life-changing events led him to discover wrong priorities and how may business people have erroneously viewed money. Questions for reflection at the end of each section make this 48-page booklet excellent for individual and group study. *softcover*

Faith & Work: Do They Mix?

Discovering God's Purposes for Your Work

When you go to work on Monday, do you take your faith with you? Hillman provides Biblical insight into God's view of work and how our faith should be integrated into all aspects of life. Hillman's practical examples from scripture and his own story will encourage you in your journey to find purpose and meaning in your work life. *softcover*

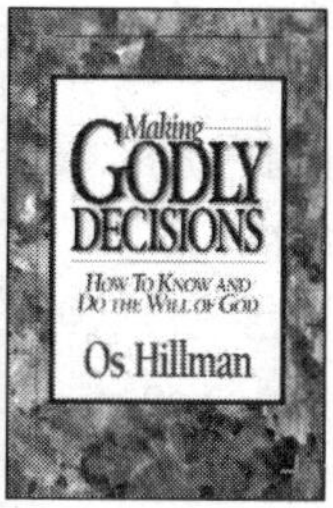

Making Godly Decisions

How To Know and Do the Will of God

In *Making Godly Decisions*, Os Hillman provides a thorough look, through scripture and personal experience, the principles for making good decisions. Hillman provides real-life case studies from others and from his own spiritual journey that will show you how to apply these principles. *softcover*

Marketplace Leaders/Aslan Group Publishing

PHONE 678-455-6262 FAX 678-455-6264 www.marketplaceleaders.org

More Resources by Os Hillman

Marketplace Mentor

Who Is Your Mentor?

Few things have been more important to Os Hillman's spiritual journey than the valuable input and direction provided by the mentors God has sent into his life. Some advised him on spiritual matters. others gave counsel on business concerns. and then a few have been simply life mentors. Their value to him could not be measured in dollars and cents. Often, he wished that God would send a mentor, gifted in all three areas—one he could retain, through a formal arrangement, to speak into his life on a regular basis. Have you ever wished for that?

Many *TGIF Today God Is First* subscribers have asked Os for more teaching and practical application of the principles found in the daily marketplace meditations. This has led us to establish the *Marketplace Mentor* program that is a twice-a-month e-Zine and contains 6-8 pages of content written by Os Hillman. It is not a one-on-one mentoring program, but it is the closest thing we could develop that is affordable and serves the most people. Each issue contains a practical workplace-focused article, tips on applying your faith in the workplace, recommended resources, profiles of workplace ministries, and other practical helps designed to help you thrive in your workplace calling. For more on this program visit our website at www. marketplaceleaders.org.

Called to the Workplace: From Esau to Joseph

How Can You Experience God In Your Work?

Why do most of us tend to segment our spiritual life from our work life? Can I really know God's will for my life? How can I make decisions that will be blessed by God? Why do most Christians in the workplace live a defeated life? *Called to the Workplace: From Esau to Joseph* 6-tape audio and workbook program is the one-day workshop that is a biblically-based leadership course which answers these and many more questions. The result of this intensive workshop helps workplace believers understand their mission and calling through the workplace. The theme of the workshop—"How To Find and Fulfill Your Destiny"—encourages you to understand your individual calling. You may also want to host this workshop at your church or workplace. Visit our website or call us to order.

Marketplace Leaders/Aslan Group Publishing

PHONE 678-455-6262 FAX 678-455-6264 www.marketplaceleaders.org

Made in the USA
Columbia, SC
14 January 2022

54288903R00071

Skip's Guide to Keeping Real Hard Cichlids™

Lawrence E. Smith

Skip's Guide to Keeping Real Hard Cichlids™

By Lawrence E. Smith

Publishing Consultant

Deborah M. Smart
http://onesmartladyproductions.com
http://www.gladstonepublishing.com
Logo Designer
Tyjae Smart

Aggression Level Chart

Charity Garrett

Power Scale/Rating System Chart

Charlene Carter

Skip's Website: www.realhardcichlids.com

Publication Date: January 2014
Imprint:
Skip's Aquarium Maintenance Services LLC

ISBN-13: 978-0-9836603-0-9
ISBN-10: 0-9836603-0-1

Made in USA

Table of Contents

1. Acknowledgements-[i]

2. Introduction-[iii]

3. Skip's Aquarium Maintenance Service
Guidelines and Instructions-[5]

4. New Tank Syndrome-[8]

6. Cloudy Water-[12]

7. Green Water: What is it and
How to get rid of it-[16]

8. Water Changes: Why, When
and How?-[19]

9. The Best Way to Lay Out an Aquarium for Large Cichlid
Communities- Aquascaping-[24]

10. Instructions to Chart/
Rating System and Power Scale-[26]

11. Aggression Level Chart-[27]

12. Rating System/Power Scale
(Strengths and Weaknesses)-[28]

13. Let's Take a Look at Target Fish for your Aggressive Cichlid Community Tank-[29]

14. Why Buy Pure Breed?-[32]

15. What's Wrong with Hybrids?-[34]

16. How to Recognize a Reputable Breeder-[36]

17. Types of Breeding-[39]

18. My Ingenious Training Method on How to Cure Shy Cichlid Behavior-[43]

19. Skip's Secret Fast Growing Cichlid-[45]

20. Common Fish Diseases-[46]

21. Let's Talk about Jaw Locking-[51]

22. Let's Take a Look at Various Real Hard Cichlids™-[53]

- Black Nasty-[53]
- Butterkofferi-[58]
- Dovii-[62]
- Friedrichstahlii-[69]
- Grammodes-[73]
- Managuense-[78]

- Midas Cichlid-[83]
- Red Tiger-[87]
- Pyro Trimac-[92]
- Umbriferum-[99]

23. Skip's Top Ten List of the Most Powerful, Toughest, Aggressive Cichlids in the World-[106]

24. Skip's Top Ten List of Overrated Aggressive and Toughest Cichlids-[107]

25. Listed are Maps Where Real Hard Cichlids™ can be Found in their Natural Environments-[108]

26. Cichlid Index-[109]

27. The Author – [111]

28. Influences-[114]

ACKNOWLEDGEMENTS

This book would have been impossible to write without the love and support of my beautiful wife Sonya Smith. Thank you; for allowing me to keep over twenty aquariums in the basement of our home without a single complaint and the many weekdays and weekends of me being absent from home to fulfill my passion. In addition, for not being upset when you saw the five aquariums in the garage; which should have been two quarantine aquariums (I know you are smiling). My gratitude and love goes out to Mrs. Gail Smith, my mother. Thank you for raising me to respect all things; especially "nature" and always encouraging me to follow my dreams. In addition, I would like to thank my buddies, Tony, Chuck, Brian and Derrick Massie for all of your support and being as

passionate about the Cichlid culture as I am. I want to THANK all of my YouTube subscribers and Facebook friends for your support and enthusiasm; because without you Real Hard Cichlids™ Aquatic Kennels could not have grown as much as it has.

Finally, to my publishing consultant, Deborah Smart, thank you for helping to bring my vision to life for me to share with all of the aquatic lovers and the rest of the world. This book was written with the presumption that the reader has a basic knowledge and understanding of owning aquariums and cichlids.

INTRODUCTION

Hi,

Let me introduce myself. My name is Lawrence Smith, better known as "Skip" a.k.a. *fishlaw1*, and one of my favorite past time hobbies is collecting tropical fish. This has been a passion of mine since 1985 and shortly thereafter, I developed an interest in breeding cichlids. What is a cichlid you might ask? A cichlid is a type of tropical freshwater and brackish water fish that is a very popular aquarium fish for homes. They currently are sold at all major pet stores that sell fish.

This is how Real Hard Cichlids™ came to life. I know you are wondering what the term "real hard cichlids" stands for. Well, let me answer that question for you. At Skip's Aquarium & Real Hard Cichlids™ Kennel, we are committed to breeding our own unique line of

cichlids combined with intelligence, toughness and high drive.

In essence, we have created the most physically impressive cichlids around. Some examples are the monster Dovi cichlids, Rampage and the mighty Chaos. My PyroMac cichlids are true old school Trimacs. Below is a breeding pair of my Super Red Tiger Motaguensis cichlids laying eggs on a rock.

Skip's Aquarium Maintenance Services Guidelines and Instructions

Maintenance for your freshwater aquarium

To assure years of enjoyment with your freshwater aquarium and proper maintenance, practice is important and will lead to a continued healthy aquarium.

Here are some helpful tips to maintain your freshwater aquarium. These guidelines are to be used every day or at the very least, every other day.

1. Feed your fish twice a day – DO NOT OVERFEED. I recommend turning the tank lights on only when feeding your fish. Leaving the tank lights on longer than one hour will lead to ex-

cess algae build up and this will cause your tank to become very unattractive between professional service periods.

2. Feed your fish the same time every day, to monitor their dietary habits.

3. Check the water temperature (suggested temperature should be between 78-80 degrees at all times).

4. Check the heater and make sure the thermostat light is working properly.

5. Make sure all filters are working properly.

6. Check for dead fish and remove immediately. Remove excess algae from glass when you see it. Algae are an organism that usually includes green, yellow-green, brown, and red fungus that grows in wet or moist areas. Example, old bread (green or blue algae grows on old bread).

7. Wipe off excess salt build-up on mechanical parts of your tank.

8. When your tank water starts to evaporate, add lukewarm tap water or room temperature spring water.

The attention you give your tank is directly linked to your dedication to maintain quality of life for your fish. Your diligence will increase the longevity of your fish, aquarium and equipment parts. The above guidelines can serve as a reminder to assure a healthy marine environment for your fish and an overall beautiful freshwater aquarium.

New Tank Syndrome

What is it and what to do about it?

What is new tank syndrome?

New tank syndrome is when an aquarium with fish has an excess of fish waste and not enough bacteria to breakdown the waste. Here is how you avoid new tank syndrome. Before you setup your aquarium, ensure that it is sterile. Next, you should add fish so they can produce fish waste.

Not to worry, because the most important fish waste you have to be concerned about is the ammonia (NH3). Ammonia is poisonous to fish and other aquatic life. Therefore, you must not allow the ammonia to build up to a concentration that is high enough to kill fish.

In nature ammonia is consumed by bacteria (nitro somas). You will use the same bacteria in your tanks to control the ammonia. When the ammonia is consumed it becomes nitrite (NO^2). The nitrite is still poisonous to the fish. You will need second bacteria (Nitro-bacteria) to convert the nitrite to harmless nitrate. The time needed for both bacteria to grow and rid the tank of toxic waste is about 4-6 weeks. When bacteria have grown, the tank is cycled.

What to do about new tank syndrome?

The only cure for new tank syndrome is to introduce bacteria into the tank. There are many ways to accomplish this. Adding bacteria from a bottled source is the easiest way. There are various bottled bacteria on the market that will seed your tank with the needed bacteria (Nitro somas) so that your tank

will cycle faster. Another way is to add used gravel from an already cycled and established tank into your new tank. The more used gravel you add to your tank the faster it will cycle.

A third way to cycle your tank is to use a dirty filter pad or sponge in your filter. This will serve as a seed-bed for the bacteria to spread to the rest of the tank. You must remember that bacteria use the ammonia, which is a "good" source; thus, if there is no "food" for the bacteria, it cannot grow. Add the bacteria only if there are already fish and ammonia in the tank.

Another helpful hint is to aerate your tank heavily while it is going through the cycle. The bacteria must have enough oxygen to convert the Ammonia to Nitrite and then to Nitrate. When there is a lack of oxygen, the time required to cycle your tank increases.

Adding an air pump or another aerating device will shorten the time needed to cycle your tank. The bacteria can only grow if the pH balance of your tank is 5.5 or higher. Below, a pH balance of 5.5, the bacteria is incapable of growing, and thus, your tank will not cycle.

The temperature of the tank's water can also play a role in the time needed to cycle your tank. The optimal temperature for bacterial growth is between 78-84 degrees Fahrenheit; therefore, make sure to have the temperature in the optimal range as suggested above.

Cloudy Water

What is it and how to get rid of it?

Why is my aquarium cloudy?

When your aquarium's water is cloudy and grey in color it means that, you have a bacterial bloom in your tank. A bacterial bloom is when the bacteria in the tank multiply at such a high rate and in such high numbers that it clouds the water.

In addition, an excess of nutrients in the water causes a bacterial bloom. Usually, the water goes cloudy when you: first set-up the aquarium, complete a water change, over-feed the fish, add new fish into the aquarium, and introduce a contaminant into the tank.

The list below details instances why your aquarium is cloudy.

When you complete a water change, the fresh water added to the tank can cause cloudiness. Over feed your fish and there may be uneaten rotten food left in the aquarium. The rotting process will release a large amount of nutrients into the water. The bacteria in the tank will use the nutrients that may cause trace elements to grow and multiply; thus contributing to the water being cloudy.

Lastly, containment of liquids chemicals and dirty hands will lead to cloudy water. Please note that in a filtered and aerated aquarium the actual bacterial bloom itself is not harmful to the fish; it is merely unsightly.

However, the actual cause of the bloom may be harmful. If the bloom is left alone; the cloudiness will go away in a few days to a few months; depending on your situation.

How do I clear the tank?

To clear the aquarium you must control the amount of nutrients in the water. Starting a new aquarium or completing a water change I recommend that you wait for the bloom to subside. It will take one to five days to clear. In the event of over feeding, I recommend that you give your tank a water change and clean the gravel thoroughly of all uneaten and floating food.

Adding a liquid bacterial supplement will help clear the tank quickly. The use of activated carbon and other chemical filtration media will also help clear the tank by removing excess nutrients from the water. After adding new fish to your tank, adding a liquid

bacterial supplement is helpful with the processing of the additional waste. However, my experience has been that completing a 100% water change can help to clear a tank immediately.

Green Water

What is it and how to get rid of it?

Why is my aquarium water green?

The water is green because of free-floating plank tonic algae in the water. Algae require light and nutrients to grow. In an average community aquarium with live plants, I recommend 10-12 hours of artificial light. In tanks without any live plants, I recommend keeping the lights on only for your viewing pleasure. Clock timers are a good way to control the duration of light. Sunlight can also cause an algae bloom.

I do not recommend that you place the aquarium in direct sunlight. Please be cautious in placing the tank in a brightly lit room, i.e. greenhouse and sunrooms, as indirect light can also cause an algae bloom. With the change in seasons, the sun's position in the sky will

change and may light the room too brightly. Another factor that can cause your water to turn green is the nutrients in the water. Nutrients in our aquariums include: fish waste, the products of decay and prepared plant fertilizers. Having too many fish in the aquarium, excess food and overdosing on prepared fertilizers are sure ways to get green water.

How do I get rid of the green water?

A sure-fire way to eradicate the green water is with the use of good algae-cede. Algae-cede come in a liquid or a tablet form. Simply follow the directions on the package. Be sure to remove the carbon and any other chemical filtration media from the filters as they will remove the algae-cede from the water.

I normally would not recommend the use of algae-cedes with live plants. In this case, I would seek out the cause of the green water. In most situations, a

combination of too much light and too much nutrients in the water is the cause of the green water. Reducing the duration and intensity of light is a way to clear the water. The use of clock timers to control the light duration is highly recommended. I also recommend draw the blinds and curtains to block sunlight. Additionally, changing the water will remove some excess nutrients. Also, during the water change do not forget to remove all excess food and to clean the filters as decaying materials in the filters will release nutrients into the aquarium. Finally, I advocate adding "Natures Best" live plants to your aquarium.

Here are the reasons why I suggest live plants: Live plants will help decrease green water, because of the following. They are more competitive than algae; are larger to provide more shade; are better at utilizing low levels of nutrients from the water, and they are beneficial at starving algae.

Real Hard Cichlids™ Kennel

Water Changes:
Why, When, and How

Why do we have to do water changes?

We complete water change to provide the fish with a clean environment to live in. Fish breathe, eat, and sleep in the same water they produce their waste. Waste build up in the tank can kill the fish. Luckily, you have good bacteria in your tanks to break down most of the waste.

Some waste cannot be broken down, so it builds up over time. If the waste concentrations become too high, the fish can die. Another reason for the water change is to prevent the pH (acidity of the water) from dropping too low. As bacteria breaks

down fish waste, acid is produced as a by-product. Over time, the pH of the tank can drop quite low. If the water becomes too acidic it will burn and kill the fish. These are the main reasons why we change the water in our fish aquariums.

Other reasons include initiation of spawning and removing of debris among many others.

When do we do water changes?

The frequency in which you complete a water change depends on how many fish, their size, the size of your aquarium, how much you feed, and what type of fish you have. A good rule to follow is water change about once every month for an average aquarium stocked moderately with small community fish. However, if you stock your aquarium more heavily, have large fish, feed more often, the frequency of water change increases. In

such cases, a water change should be completed once every two weeks or even once a week. Certain types of fish require very clean water. "Beani's cichlid" is such a fish. To keep these fish, a weekly water change may be necessary. Ask me for my recommendations for your specific cichlid or aquarium.

How do we complete water changes?

Before you start the removal of water from your tank, first prepare the water that is going into your tank. Allow the new water to sit out overnight or use a de-chlorinate. I don't recommend that you mix hot and cold water; even though the temperature will be in the proper range, because there will be too much dissolved gas in the water. the dissolved gas is seen as bubbles that form on the sides of the glass or container holding the water.

The dissolved gas can kill your fish by entering the fish's body and then forming bubbles inside the fish. This is similar to a scuba diver surfacing too quickly.

In the summer time, the water can be used immediately after a de-chlorinator is added. However, I still recommend that you allow the water to sit out overnight. The actual water change involves removing up to 50% of the aquarium's water.

Remember to leave the fish in the water during the change, but remove all ornaments. I recommend cleaning with a siphon gravel cleaner, because it systematically cleans the entire gravel bed. Try to remove as much debris from the gravel as possible. Don't worry about taking out too much dirt, as you can never remove all of it. Ask me to show you how to use a siphon gravel cleaner and

how to clean the gravel properly. After the change, replace the water with treated water.

The Best Way to Lay Out an Aquarium for Large Cichlid Communities

Aquascaping

First scatter large smooth pebbles in a group to form "association" areas for the fish, next arrange large boulder and/or slates to form a natural series of caves. Large cichlids can easily dislodge stones and cause damage to the aquarium glass try to ensure

that the rocks are stable. A Beachwood branch and a large piece of dogwood create a focal point in the design. Behind the dogwood, use a power head to direct water flow to the front of the tank so that it makes for a beautiful aquarium.

Instructions to Chart/Rating System and Power Scale

The following is a breakdown of my rating system for Cichlid levels of aggression. This chart ranges from a low 1 to a top 5 which gives an indication of the species aggression levels. Rating at a level one is "non-aggressive" and a rating at a level five is "highly aggressive." For example, a Cichlid typically loses one rating point if it is shy, easily startled or afraid of its tank mates.

The following is a tool that I use to showcase the different strength and weakness/power scale for Cichlids. The table indicates the difference between delicate Cichlids and hardy Cichlids and each color code represents the difference between strong and weak species.

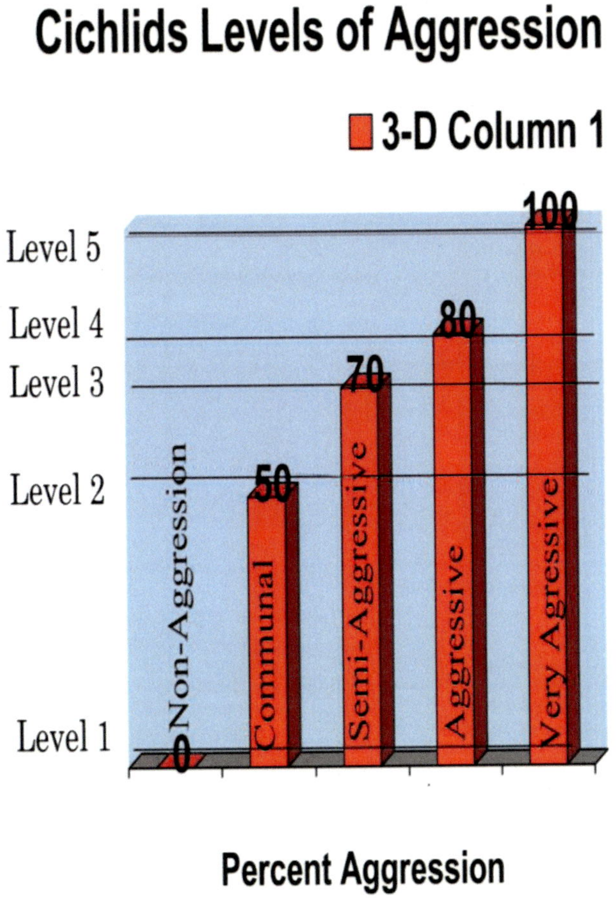
Cichlids Levels of Aggression
3-D Column 1
Level 5
Level 4
Level 3
Level 2
Level 1
0
50
70
80
100
Non-Aggression
Communal
Semi-Aggressive
Aggressive
Very Agressive
Percent Aggression

BREAKDOWN OF CICHLID SPECIES
STRENGTHS VS. WEAKNESSES
RATING SYSTEM

	Yellow	Orange	Green	Red
LIFE EXPECTANCY	4-7 Years	8-10 Years	10-12 Years	12-20 Years
DIET	Too much protein based food can cause blockage of the intestinal tract area which can cause bloating	Flexible feeding (Omnivore)	Good appetite; very few foods can cause digestive problems	Flexible feeding (Omnivore) (Can eat almost anything)
ACCLIMATING TO WATER CHANGES	Most of these species do not adapt to water changes well	These species moderately adapt to most water changes	These species generally adapt easily to water changes	These species adapt easily to water changes.
DEALING WITH TANK-MATES: LEVELS OF AGRESSION	Will not get along well with other fish	Can be kept with other fish if constantly observed	Can be kept with other cichlids of equal size only	These species are best left in the tank by themselves
PHYSICALLY POWERFUL; CAPABLE OF EXERTING GREAT PHYSICAL FORCE AND POWER (SCALE OF 1-10 -- 1-LOW & 10 HIGH)	4	6	8	10

Let's Take a Look at Target Fish for Your Aggressive Cichlid Community Tank

First, what is a target fish? The ideal target fish is a hardy fish built like a tank, fast and agile, and somewhat expendable. The role of the target fish is to act as a decoy in the tank to help vent both territorial and breeding aggression. Since, the average target fish is faster than any of its cichlid tank mates it can handle high speed chases and will more likely escape without harm.

A benefit of using a target fish is that it gives the usually dominant male of a breeding pair of cichlids, a diversion and thus keeps his spouse from taking the brunt of the males' territorial and sexual frustration.

Target fish will also induce better fry defense in species that offer any. Here are a few listed commonly used target fish: large Tin-foil bard, Silver Dollars, Zebra Danios and the giant Pearl Dianios. These fish are generally readily available reasonable and very efficient swimmers. Additionally these fish are very adaptable in terms of water conditions so they can be used in a broad range of cichlid community tanks.

Tinfoil Barbs

Silver Dollars

Why Buy A Pure-Breed?

Buying purebred cichlids increases the consumer chances of receiving healthy and quality cichlids. Be careful when choosing your breed, because there are many popular crossbred cichlids on the market, which are often sold as pure-breeds. For an example, Flower horn cichlids that sometimes pass for purebred Trimac cichlids.

Do not be afraid to ask the breeder for their breed standards and by doing this you will have knowledge of their major/minor flaws within their bloodline. Every good breeder should have a breed standard and know their pedigrees.

What is wrong with Hybrids?

1. Hybrids are often sold as pure-breeds and many people have been misled; because hybrids appear to be authentic and this is why it is a bad idea.

2. Some people breed hybrids and their fry are born looking very different from what they expected.

3. Purebred cichlids suffer when you cross-breed.

4. You cannot find too many purebred Trimac cichlids anymore, because some cichlid hobbyists are only concern with making money.

Take a look at the Hybrid below.

How to Recognize a Reputable Breeder

Listed below are important characteristics of a reputable breeder.

1. Reputable breeders only produce a spawn with the goal of improving their breed and with the full intent of keeping a fish from the spawn to continue their efforts. They do not breed to make money to supply the pet market during a wave of breed popularity, or simply, because they happen to have two cichlids of the same breed on the premises. If the breeder has produced a spawn for a crazy reason, beware!

2. Reputable breeders belong to a local or national Cichlid club and are actively showing fish.

3. Reputable breeders are willing and eager to spend time with you explaining, teaching, and advising the consumer about their breed of cichlids.

4. Reputable breeders stay in touch with you on a regular basis to assess how your fish is adapting. They do not disappear.

Remember, it is up to you, the consumer to make your choice wisely and to do your homework. You have to inspect what you expect when buying cichlids. Talk at length with as many breeders as possible, quiz each one about

their breed, and look at many fish. A reputable breeder will be impressed and reassured that you are concerned about what you are doing rather than impulse buying. Find a breeder with whom you are comfortable, whose fish you like, and pick out your dream cichlid. Results, everybody wins! Breeders must produce the best product to be in the reordering business and not the sales business.

Remember people, you must inspect what you expect when buying Cichlids.

Types of Breeding

1. **Line breeding** is a form of inbreeding practiced by some cichlid breeders to "fix" desirable strains in a breed of fish or animal without a high risk of producing undesirable traits that may occur with close inbreeding. An example of line breeding would be considered as mating of first cousins or more distantly related individuals who share a common ancestor. While line breeding is less likely to cause problems in the first generation than inbreeding, over time line breeding can reduce the genetic diversity of a population. This causes problems related to a too small gene pool that may include an increased prevalence of genetic disorders and inbreeding depression.

2. **Selective Line Breeding** is the process of breeding fish and animals for particular genetic traits. Typically, strains which are selectively bred are domesticated, and the breeding is sometimes done by a professional breeder. Bred cichlids are known as breeds, while bred plants are known as varieties, cultigens, or cultivars. To cross-breed two types of species of fish is called "hybrids". The term selective breeding is synonymous with artificial selection.

3. **Out crossing** is the practice of introducing unrelated genetic material into a breeding line. It increases genetic diversity, thus reducing the probability of all individuals being subject to disease or reducing genetic abnormalities; "only within the first generation." Out crossing

can serve to increase the number of individuals who carry a disease recessively. It is used in line breeding to restore vigor, size, and fertility to a breeding line.

4. **Inbreeding** is reduced fitness in a given population as a result of breeding related individuals. Breeding between closely related individuals is called *inbreeding*. This inbreeding causes recessive deleterious traits manifesting themselves. The more closely related the breeding pair is the more homozygous the genes offspring.

5. **Heterosis Hybridizing** is a term used in genetics and selective breeding. The term heterocyst, also known as "Hybrid Vigor" or out breeding enhancement, describes the increased strength of different characteristics in hybrids the possi-

bility to obtain a genetically superior individual by combining the virtues of its parents. Heterosis or Hybridizing is the opposite of inbreeding depression, which occurs with increasing homozygosis. The term often causes controversy, particularly in terms of the selective breeding of domestic animals, because it is sometimes believed that all crossbred fish or animals are genetically superior to their parents. This is true only in certain circumstances. When a hybrid is seen to be superior to its parents this is known as hybrid vigor. The opposite happens when a hybrid inherits traits from their parents this makes them unfit for survival and the result is referred as out breeding depression. An example of this is a cross between wild and hatchery fish that have incompatible adoptions.

My Ingenious Training Method on How to Cure Shy Cichlid Behavior

1. You should always feed your fish with the light on in your aquarium so that he or she can get familiar with you at all times.

2. You should always hold your hands and arms above the tank for one minute when feeding them.

3. Always let your fish see your face when greeting them.

4. Use their natural instincts to defend their territory by placing a mirror in front of them so that they see their image reflecting back at them.

Take a mirror and move it from time to time around the front of your aquarium so that the fish follow its movements.

5. When your fish start to follow the mirror consistently, replace the mirror with your hand. Once your fish start chasing your hand, reward them with food.

Now you have a well-trained fish that will no longer be shy or scared of you anymore.

Enjoy!

Skip's Secret Fast Growing Cichlid Methods

1. **Tank size:** your tank should be between 50 and 125 gallons. (This includes breeder size tanks as well).
2. **Water Changes:** you should change 1/3 or 1/2 of your water twice a month.
3. **Temperature:** the temperature in your aquarium should be between 75-80 degrees Fahrenheit.
4. **Power Feeding:** You should feed your fish three times a day until, they reach adult size. Once at the adult size, start once a day feeding. A suggested blend of fish food is Real Hard Cichlids™' special blend, night crawlers; which is high in protein, spirulina and veggie matter.

Common Fish Diseases

I make no claim that I am an expert on cichlid diseases. However, my experience and philosophy is "if you complete water changes consistently along with using a good filtration system the chances of disease are lowered." It is my opinion that the more common the cichlid the smaller chance of diseases; particularly Central American cichlids like Real Hard Cichlids™.

Cichlid Rubbing

If your cichlids are rubbing against the aquarium glass or ornaments, you should complete a 30% water change; service the filter, vacuum the gravel to remove the accumulated crud and check the nitrates levels. Once this is completed, add a teaspoon of rock salt per ten gallons of water to aid the fish to create a protective slime on their skin.

Ich

What is Ich?

Ich is a protozoan disease that is often called "white spot disease."

What does Ich look like?

Ich looks like a fine dusting of sugar covering all or part of the fish.

How to cure Ich?

The key to treating Ich is to act quickly (the minute you see it). If you wait a day or two the game is often over. There are various brands of Ich medicine and all requires treatment of the aquarium daily with a number of drops of the liquid medicine. You must treat the aquarium everyday for the

whole period suggested on the bottle *(this is often for a week)*. The treatment works because everyday some of the cysts are hatching and the treatment kills that day's parasites. Ich is cured faster if treated with warm water.

Hint: "Keeping a bottle of Ich medicine around the house is a good idea."

The spots on this cichlid looks like Ich, but it is not Ich. This is a Polleni cichlid from Manugasce Africa.

Pop Eye

Pop Eye is also known as exophthalmoses or exophthalmia. This subject matter is often confusing, because Pop Eye is more of a bacterial infection rather than a disease. In fresh water fish the infection may affect one of both eyes appearing as if the eye has air or fluid trapped inside, around, or behind it; causing the eye to enlarge and bulge out of its socket; as if

under pressure. The duration of this condition can be anywhere from several days to several weeks. If your fish is still eating, I recommend feeding it a medicated food (for bacterial infections). I have had limited success by combing Naladixic Acid and Kanamycin Sulfate. Pop Eye usually appears after the disease is far advanced and is difficult to treat.

Treatment of Pop Eye

Placing the afflicted fish into a quarantine aquarium will allow it time away from its tank mates. Pop Eye must be treated immediately if the fish is to survive.

Let's Talk About Jaw-Locking

Jaw-locking is dangerous; because the jaws are essential for many aspects of a cichlid's life. A dislocated jaw could be a prelude to death. However, jaw-locking is also the ultimate way for two closely matched cichlids to determine who wins or who loses. Jaw-locking is a very important part of cichlid culture, because it is a part of survival and courtship. Potential mates lock jaws and test their fighting ability. A partner that cannot fight is a partner that will not be able to protect their fry adequately.

Below Are Two Cichlids Jaw-Locking

Let's Take a Look at Various Real Hard Cichlids™

Black Nasty Haitiensis

Grave Digger

Scientific Name:	Haitiensis
Common Name:	Black Nasty Cichlid
Origin:	Haiti
Max Size:	14 inches
Life Span:	4-7 years

Temperature: 73-82 Fahrenheit

Minimum Tank Size: 90 gallons

Foods: Live worms, shrimp, fish, beef hearts, and pellets

Possible Tank Mates: None

The (Black Nasty) aggression level is 4.

Strengths vs. Weaknesses Rating

Delicate

Black Nasty Haitiensis

These fish are omnivores and will accept all foods offered. Their diet should be varied, but should include some vegetable matter.

Origin: Found in rivers and lakes of Haiti, and can be hard to sex. The female genitalia are larger than the males and the females can be slightly smaller. Sometimes, adult males will develop a nuchal hump on the forehead. Pairing these fish is a hard task; because sometimes the male will kill the female. The use of a tank divider is recommended in-between spawn

ing. The eggs will be laid on a flat surface; normally about 150 per batch. The female will take care of the fry for the first couple months of life.

Lifespan: Expected lifespan usually averages five years.

Black Nasty Haitiensis

In case you are not familiar with this fish, here are a couple of quick facts:

The largest male I have ever seen was about 14 inches, but they should grow to be 16 inches. Males also get a tombstone hump when mature. The largest female I have seen was also about 10 inches. Although this is a Nandopsis species, it is not nearly as aggressive as Dovii, Red Devils, or Black Belts. I hope you get the chance to keep and enjoy this fish some day.

Tilapia Butterkofferi

Scientific Name:	Tilapia Butterkofferi
Common Name:	Butter aka The Big Tilapia
Origin:	West African Cichlid
Max Size:	16 inches
Life Span:	10-15 years
Temperature:	73-82 Fahrenheit

Minimum Tank

Size: 90 gallons

Foods: Live worms, shrimp, fish, beef hearts, and pellets

Possible Tank

Mates: A fish of equal size.

The (Butter) aggression level is 5 which is the highest level.

Strengths vs. Weaknesses Rating

Hardy

Tilapia Butterkofferi

The Butterkofferi Cichlid, also known as the Zebra Tilapia, comes from the river systems of Western Africa. The coloration of this fish is a series of black and white vertical stripes. Although it can be peaceful when young, as it grows, so does its disposition, which becomes very territorial. Currently, the Butterkofferi Cichlid is successfully bred in farms and aquariums. Like all Tilapia, these fish are mouth brooders. The female will carry the eggs in her mouth for a period of several weeks depending on the temperature and then release the fry into the aquarium.

Tilapia Butterkofferi are extremely intelligent and aggressive fish.

Aquarium owners find that they are very active and react to movements outside of the aquarium, including attempts to attack an "invader" through the glass of the tank. It is generally advised not to mix them with other fish, as they can be very aggressive, with few exceptions. Butterkofferi require tanks of at least 100 gallons and temperatures of about 75-80 degrees Fahrenheit. They love all foods and need frequent water changes, because they are such big eaters.

The Awesome
Dovii Cichlid Rampage

Scientific Name:	Parachromis Dovii
Common Name:	Dovii aka Wolf Cichlid the true Guapote, Rainbow Bass Cichlid
Origin:	Central America, Honduras, Costa Rica, Nicaragua
Max Size:	28 inches, Females, 14 inches
Life Span:	10-18 years

Temperature: 73-82 F

Minimum Tank Size: 180 gallons

Foods: Live worms, shrimp, fish, beef hearts, and fish pellets.

Possible Tank Mates: None (These species are usually best left in a tank by itself.)

The (Dovii) aggression level is 5 which is the highest level.

Strengths vs. Weaknesses Rating

Dominant

Here is a photo of the very young Dovii cichlid

Metallica

The Dovii aka
the Wolf Cichlid

The adults are quite easy to sex and the juvenile specimens are not interesting. Their color is silver with a broken horizontal stripe running along the flanks; as they mature males develop longer more pointed fins that have many black spots. Males also have many small spots on their heads. Females on the other hand, rarely show any spots at all and their base color matures to mustard yellow. This species color often varies and sometimes the males have a purple base color.

Males grow much bigger than females with a much more powerful head. This is the largest Central American cichlid. The Parachromis Dovii is a pure predator in its natural habitat and is rarely interested in eating

anything other than other fish. Furthermore, the adult fish does not hide from its prey, but roams about openly in extremely clear and very clean waters. Small Wolf cichlids cannot roam; because they could become a meal for the larger ones.

Aquarium Set-Up

With a fish this size, consider first the tank size. While Dovii's are comfortable in groups in tanks of 75 to 100 gallons when they are small, they will soon require much larger accommodations. A full-grown male will need a minimum of 180 gallons or bigger. Females do not require quite the same space. However, they will not be comfortable in less than 90 gallons.

As Dovii's reach maturity at around 5 inches, their aggressive nature is displayed and groups will need to be separated. Tank mates are no good for Dovii's, as they will kill anything small enough to fit in their mouths and tear apart anything too big to get down in one gulp.

Few people have been successful in keeping breeding pairs of dovii together without a problem, but this has only been accomplished in tanks of over 200 gallons and is considered a rare occurrence.

Costa Rican Blue Dovii Cichlid

Sexing Dovii Cichlids

Males have black pepper spots all over their bodies, and females have a yellow colored with a blue or green face. The males are generally more colorful than females. These fish will breed in captivity.

Below is a picture of my Dovii

Chaos

Friedrichstahlii

Scientific Name:	Parachromis Friedrichstahlii
Origin:	Central America, Mexico, Guatemala
Temperature:	73-82 Fahrenheit
Foods:	Live worms, shrimp, fish, beef hearts, and pellets
Possible Tank Mates:	Other cichlids of equal size.

The (Friedrichstahlii) aggression level is 3

Strengths vs. Weaknesses Rating

Moderate

Common Name:	Freddy Cichlid, Yellow-Jacket Cichlid
Family:	Cichlid
Maximum Size:	10 inches for females and 12 inches for males
Life Span:	15 plus years
Origin:	Central America; From Southern Mexico to Guatemala and Belize
Minimum Tank Size:	75 gallons
Water Region:	All

Temperature: 72-80 degrees Fahrenheit. The Freddy is very tolerant of a fairly wide range of temperatures.

Water pH: 7.0-8.0

Diet: Piscivore. In the wild, the Freddy cichlid is an enthusiastic predator feeding mostly on smaller fish and invertebrates. In a home aquarium, Freddies should be provided with a diverse diet of pellets, food sticks along with live, frozen or freeze-dried foods.

Temperament: Extremely aggressive. The Freddy is not as aggressive as its larger cousins, the Managuense, the Motaguensis, and the Dovii, but the Freddy is not a wimp.

Description: Freddy cichlids have a distinctive yellow base coloration with black banding that stretches the length of their bodies. The combination of yellow

and the black bars give it the look of a Yellow Jacket hence the name Yellow Jacket Cichlid.

Sexing: Male Freddies will grow larger than females.

Breeding: A Freddy pair will form around 4-6 inches. The female will guard the eggs and then fry while the male will guard the surrounding area. Once paired, Freddies will meticulously guard the eggs and fry, and will injure or kill any fish that gets too close to the nesting area.

Grammodes Cichlid

Scientific Name:	Grammodes
Common Name:	The Little Dovii cichlid
Origin:	Central America, Pacific Slope
Max Size:	12 inches
Life Span:	8-10 years
Temperature:	73-82 Fahrenheit

Minimum Tank

Size: 55 gallons

Foods: Live worms, shrimp, fish, beef hearts, and pellets

Possible Tank

Mates: Other cichlids of equal size

The (Grammodes) aggression level is 5 which is the highest level.

Strengths vs. Weaknesses Rating

Hardy

Temperament: Aggressive and territorial, these Cichlids can be placed in a grow-out tank as juveniles with other small cichlids. However, Grammodes will have to be separated at around 4 to 6 inches.

Diet: Carnivore

Care: Grammodes are avid Piscivore in nature and a large portion of their diet is live fish. In an aquarium, tank-raised feeders can be given as a treat preferably no more than once a week. More nutritional foods would include a high quality cichlid pellet, shrimp pellet, krill pellet, and even the occasional spirulina or veggie pellet for proper balanced nutrition. Frozen or freeze dried treats of blood worms, brine shrimp, beef heart, or krill can be given as well as live treats.

Gender: Can be difficult to determine unless a group of 6 or more are avail-able for comparison. Males will have very pronounced red spots all

over their body while the female will have very few red spots below the mid-lateral line. Also, males will grow larger and develop a nuchal hump.

Breeding: This is not a common available species nor commonly spawned. A pair should form once they reach a size somewhere in the area of 4 to 6 inches at which any other fish in the tank will most likely need to be removed. A flat surface, which could be either the walls of a cave or a flat piece of slate, will be cleaned and the female will lay eggs. Once the pair has spawned, one must keep a watchful eye on the pair to make sure they do not become aggressive with each other.

Variants: The Grammodes have often been referred to as a miniature version of Parachromis Dovii and should be treated as such. A miniature means the Grammodes will only grow to a modest 12 inches instead of 30 plus inches of the real Wolf cichlid. This species is a member of the "Grammodes Complex" which also includes C. Beani and C. Istlanum. These 3 species are currently classified as ex-Cichlasoma until further study and classification can be done.

Managuense

Scientific Name:	Managuense
Common Name:	Jag
Origin:	Central America, Eastern Honduras, Lake Nicaragua
Max Size:	16 inches
Life Span:	10-20 years
Temperature:	73-82 Fahrenheit

Minimum
Tank of Size: 75 gallons

Foods: Live worms, shrimp, fish, beef hearts, and pellets

Possible
Tank Mates: Other cichlids of equal size

The (Jag) aggression level is 5 which is the highest level.

Strengths vs. Weaknesses Rating

Hardy

Family: Parachromis

Managuense

The Managuense Cichlid, also known as the Aztec Cichlid and the Jaguar Cichlid is a beautifully marked cichlid. Young Managuense cichlids are dull, silver, and gold with spots running along their bodies. As they mature the dullness is even greater. Once they are sexually mature, their drab blotches become darker; eventually turning black with an irregular pattern like that of a jaguar cat. The background color is pearly with a light purple cast. These spots are less extreme in females. The lower lip often extends up over the upper lip sometimes revealing some of the front teeth.

As a juvenile, the Managuense cichlid can be housed in a 50-gallon minimum aquarium. The adult requires an aquarium no smaller than 70 gallons. They require plenty of open swimming room,

as well as places to hide. The bottom of the tank should be coarse gravel without plants; because the Managuense cichlid is a burrower and will tear up plants.

Although this cichlid is a predator; it can be housed with other large cichlids, but sometimes will not tolerate other cichlids that are similar in color. Any fish that will fit into its mouth should not be kept in the same aquarium with the Managuense cichlid.

The male is generally larger and has pointed dorsal and anal fins as well as being more brightly colored. Breeding in an aquarium is often difficult; however, Managuense cichlids are excellent parents and form nuclear families. The female can spawn up to 5,000 yellow eggs.

The Managuense Cichlid is omnivorous and will eat most prepared frozen foods; including freeze-dried bloodworms, tubifex, ocean plankton, and flake food and cichlid pellets.

Midas Citrinellus

Scientific Name:	Aphilophus Citrinellum
Common Name:	Midas
Origin:	Central America, Guatemala, Honduras
Max Size:	14 inches
Life Span:	10-12 years
Temperature:	73-82 Fahrenheit

Minimum Tank

Size:	75 gallons
Foods:	Live worms, shrimp, fish, beef hearts, and pellets

Possible Tank

Mates:	Other cichlid of equal size

The (Midas) aggression level is 5 which is the highest level.

Strengths vs. Weaknesses Rating

Hardy

The scientific name for the Midas Cichlid is Aphilophus Citrinellum and it belongs to the cichlid family. Their natural habitats are in lakes and rivers of Costa Rica and Nicaragua. The Midas Cichlid will eat small fish, snails, plant material, and almost anything that can fit into its mouth.

The Midas Cichlid has orange and white blotchy skin with a very pronounced hump on its forehead. The Midas Cichlid is one of the largest cichlids and can grow up to 14 inches. An aquarium tank of at least 90 gallons is required to keep this fish. A very thick glass is needed, because Midas Cichlids can be aggressive and are capable of breaking an aquarium.

Midas Cichlids will eat any aquarium foods, such as live foods, frozen dried foods, flakes, and fresh vegetables. Beef heart and live worms is a favorite of these cichlids. It is possible to breed Midas Cichlids,

but aggression can pose a risk. A very large aquarium is needed, because these fish become more aggressive during spawning and egg guarding. Midas Cichlids offer great parent care so it is best to leave the fry in the same tank with their parents.

Red Tiger Motaguensis

Scientific Name:	Motaguensis
Common Name:	Red Tiger
Origin:	Central America, Guatemala, Honduras
Max Size:	12 inches
Life Span:	10 years
Temperature:	73-82 Fahrenheit

Minimum Tank Size:	75 gallons
Foods:	Live worms, shrimp, fish, beef hearts, and pellets
Possible Tank Mates:	Other cichlids of equal size

The (Red Tiger) aggression level is 4

Strengths vs. Weaknesses Rating

Hardy

Red Tiger Motaguensis

The *parachromis motaguensis* is a large bulky cichlid originating from the Central American regions of Guatemala. Unlike its close relative the *parachromis maguensis* (commonly known and traded as the jaguar cichlid), the Motaguensis is not as commonly encountered in the aquarium trade as other cichlids.

Although their visually very similar, the Motaguensis is traded by the name (Red Tiger) and is known to display an array of bright red dots; which runs along the flanks to the base of the caudal fin. An impressive array of this coloration is distinct on the gills of this fish where such color is highly pronounced.

The female of this species is colored with deep hues of reds and oranges displayed much more prominently than the male's color. This color is enhanced further during the breeding period.

Sexing

Females are smaller than the male and the red pigment seems more prominent in the gill

plates. The red coloration is significantly prominent in the female in breeding colors. The male's dorsal and ventral fins are also much more extended and elongated than the females.

Water Chemistry

The pH of 7.0-8.0 is preferable and the temperature of 27 degrees Celsius.

Trimaculatum aka PyroMac

Big King Max and Mystic

Scientific Name: Amphilophus Trimaculatum

Common Name: Trimac, three spot cichlids

Distribution: Central America, Mexico, Guatemala, And El Salvador

Max Size: 16 inches

Life Span: 10-15

Temperature: 73-82 F

Minimum Tank Size: 75 gallons

Foods: Live worms, shrimp, fish, beef hearts, and fish pellets.

Possible Tank Mates: None

The (PyroMac) aggression level is 5 which is the highest level.

Strengths vs. Weaknesses Rating

Hardy

Trimaculatum

Breeding

Generally the males will have longer fin extensions with deeper and starker looking spots than females. Females will usually show a black spot on their dorsal fin. They become sexually mature around 20cm (8 inches) in length and are open spawners who guard their spawning sites with extreme aggression. Unfortunately for this species their amaz-

ing contrasting, beautiful coloring, relatively easy cross spawning abilities, are highly hybridized for that sad money making machine which is known as the Flowerhorn trade. The harm to Trimacs at this level is due to the lower grade Flowerhorns often being bred back to the original Trimac line. This pollutes the gene pool and these fish are sold as pure Trimacs, which they are not. The Central American Cichlid known as the (Pyro Trimac) is also referred to as Pyromac. The scientific name is (Cichlasoma Trimaculatum). The Pyromac was bred in Real Hard Cichlids™ Kennel in Prince George's County, Maryland in the year 2004.

The PyroMac strain is a true Trimac that is a result of breeding two different types of Trimacs into one. The first is a true Green Trimac; the second is the true Gold Trimac, which equals 100% pure Trimac cichlid

breeds. There are two different types of Trimac species to make one super Trimac. The Super Trimac is not a new breed, but an old breed long forgotten in the cichlid world until now.

I, Skip, better known as Fishlaw1, will bring the Super Trimac back. The authentic Trimac is from the Pacific slope of Mexico to El Salvador and not from Asia. The hybrid Flowerhorn (fancy name for a crossbreed) comes from Far East where most fish are bred in an effort to increase sales.

These fish are not naturally bred; they are test tube babies like the Blood Parrot fish, Rose Queen, and Pearl horn; which are bred in fish labs on farms in Malaysia by crossing several different species of fish. You should not crossbreed a fish that inhabits in a lake in one part of the world with a fish in another part of the world; because they are cichlids genetically. They

are not the same species; therefore, the results are mutated offspring's. Why disturb nature's beautiful fish?

You can always breed two of the same species just like the common Oscar and the Red Oscar, thus creating the Tiger Oscar. Breeding the pair creates an Oscar. However, when two different species of fish are crossbred and the consumer goes to purchase a particular breed of fish such as the Trimac and takes it home to breed is when the problem begins. You arrive home to breed with the Trimac (you thought you purchased); however, what was created was an offspring given the false impression of a Red Devil or something else. The genetics are not compatible leading to a shorten lifespan for the fish. Now, if you are willing to pay top dollar for a crossbreed hybrid; what are you willing to pay for a true 100% purebred Trimac with natural Red, Green, Golden, and Blue colors made in the

USA? Crossbreeding ends up in disaster by confusing the consumer and hobbyists.

Hint: Consumers want to know what they are getting. Crossbreeding of cichlids MUST stop (they are Frankenstein lab-made fish). Here is a great example of what I do. Trimac makes one Pyromac, and I call the two combined species Pyromac; because the word Pyro means "fire or heat," which will result in a reddish gold-blue color that are on their fins and body. The word Tri- means "three spots or occurring in intervals of three." The word Mac means "massive, enlarged, and green" (Hulk-like); thus, the PyroMac cichlid. My cichlids are raised naturally in a controlled environment to help decrease crossbreeding.

Umbriferum

Big Zeus at 22 inches

Scientific
Name: Caquetaia Umbriferus

Distribution: South America Colombia and Panama river basins

Size: Males –Up to 24 inches (61 cm) and females up to 13 inches (33cm)

Common Names: Umbee, Blue-freckled monster,

Life Span: 10-15 years

Minimum Tank Size: 180 gallons

Foods: Live worms, shrimp, fish, beef hearts, and pellets

Possible Tank Mates: None

The (Umbee) aggression level is 5 which is the highest level.

Strengths vs. Weaknesses Rating

Dominant

Temperature: 72-80 degrees Fahrenheit (22-27 degrees Celsius)

Umbree Cichlids

General Characteristic: With this cichlid, the name pretty much says it all. Blue-freckled MONSTER!!! With males around 24 inches (61 cm), the Umbee is one of the largest cichlids available in the Cichlid hobby and is considered by many to be equal only to the Dovii in aggressiveness and appetite. Males generally have a dull brownish-gold base color

with scarlet blush on their heads. The vibrantly iridescent blue "freckles" on the face and gill plates are what give this fish its distinctive common name.

The dorsal, caudal, and tailfins show a spectacular shade of blue and often hints of green. Females are generally a little more on the bland size; however, they still show the brilliant blue facial freckles and blue/green coloration on their dorsal and tailfins.

Adult males are sometimes described as "all muscle," mouth and attitude classifying these fish as a real favorite for those wanting larger aggressive cichlids. Be warned, as with Doviis, these fish will consider a large area of space around their

tank as part of their territory and will regularly charge at the glass to dispel the invaders, be they animal, vegetable, or mineral in nature.

Breeding: Breeding Umbees can be quite a challenge, as they are not tolerant of their own kind. Given the size difference between a full-grown male and female, attempts can often lead to heartbreak. With these fish it is a better idea to spawn them through a divider, where eggs can be fertilized without the female being at risk from the male's wrath. Spawning in this fashion is not the most practical or the most productive form of breeding, but it is far safer than risking your female. As with most cichlids the female lays her eggs on a flat

rock which one or more parents have cleaned beforehand. After fertilization takes place, the female guards the eggs while the male patrols and defends the territory. Both fish will be at their most territorial at this stage, and care should be taken not to disturb them; unless you are not fond of your fingers. With the amount of power a male Umbee has at his disposal, he can do major damage to your fingers and fish.

The 12" Female Umbee Sky

Real Hard Cichlid™ Kennel

Skip's Top 10 List of the Most Powerful and Toughest Aggressive Cichlids in the World

1. Dovii – aka Wolf Cichlid
2. Pyro Trimac – aka the authentic Teardrop Cichlid
3. Umbriferum – aka the Blue Freckled Monster
4. Managuense – aka the Jaguar Cichlid
5. Butterkofferi – aka the Big Tilapia
6. Motaguensis – aka the Red Tiger Cichlid
7. Blue Devil/Bar – aka The Midas Cichlid
8. Grammodes – aka the Little Dovii Cichlid
9. Istlanum – aka The Red Rio Amacuzac Cichlid
10. Jack Dempsey – aka Famous Boxer 1920

Real Hard Cichlids™ Kennel

Skip's Top 10 List of Overrated Aggressive & Toughest Cichlids in the World

1. Beani – aka Little Diamond
2. Haitiensis – aka Black Nasty
3. Festae – aka True Red Terror
4. Cuban Cichlid
5. Bleekeri – aka Large Spot
6. Polleni – aka Small Spot
7. Oscar
8. Texas Cichlid
9. Green Terror
10. Splendida – aka Red Snook

Listed are Maps Where Real Hard Cichlids™ can be Found in their Natural Environment

Cichlid Index

Common Names	Scientific Names	Page Numbers
Black Nasty	Haitiensis	53, 107
Butta	Butterkofferi	58, 106
Wolf Cichlid	Dovii	iv, 62, 64, 67, 68, 106
Freddy Cichlid	Friedrichstahlii	69, 72
Little Dovii	Grammodes	73, 106
Jagua Cichlid	Managuense	78, 106
Midas Cichlid	Citrinellum	83, 106
Red Tiger	Motaguensis	87, 89, 106
Pyro Trimac	Trimaculatum	32, 92, 94, 106
Umbee	Umbriferum	99, 101, 106

Cichlid Index (cont'd)

Condition or Example	Name	Page Numbers
Target Fish	Tinfoil Barbs, Silver Dollars	31
Hybrids		35
Ich-like Spots but not Ich	Polleni Cichlids	48, 107
Pop-Eye Bacterial Infection		49
Lock-Jawing		51, 52

The Author

Lawrence Smith aka "Skip" was born and raised in Washington, DC. He was five years old when he received his first five-gallon fish bowl. He received a gold fish that he and his mother named "Big Fish." It was love at first sight for him and at that very moment, his passion for fish developed. At age fifteen he was introduced to Cichlids by his childhood friend named Bill. Skip's first Cichlid was a "Red Oscar" the most popular Cichlid in all of the local pet stores at that time. His passion continued to intensify with the acquiring of different types of Cichlids such as: Jack Dempseys, Convicts and Red Devils. He began to save his school lunch money and took many trips down to Larry's Fish Bowl located in Northeast Washington, DC to purchase

his Cichlids. This was the birth of his Cichlid hobby. Years later his beloved uncle "Sterling" (Rest in Peace) introduced him to a man named Demus, aka; "The Godfather of Cichlids." Demus was called "The Godfather of Cichlids;" because he owned a vast variety of Cichlids such as: Doviis, Umbees, Trimacs and many others. During the 1980's and 1990's those Cichlids were considered rare in the DC Metropolitan area and were difficult to acquire. His interest and passion developed into a beloved business known as "Skips Aquarium Maintenance Services, LLC." His experience in the business with Local Pet Stores, Churches, Funeral Homes, Barber Shops, Law Offices and personal clients created a demand to obtain rare Cichlids for their aquariums. Raising and breeding his own rare Cichlids, he was able to meet the needs of his clients; thus, the creation of Real Hard Cichlids™

Aquatic Kennels came to life. Skip's Aquarium Maintenance Services, LLC and Real Hard Cichlids™ Aquatic Kennels mission is to show that the Cichlid hobby can be fulfilling and rewarding. Lastly, his desire is to expose children, adolescent, as well as, others to this very fulfilling hobby. Skip's plan is to be a leading example of how to embrace aquatic life.

Influences

Larry owner of "Larry's Fish Bowl"

Otis aka Big O

from"Larry's Fish Bowl"

Demus aka

"The Godfather of Cichlids"

Don Conkel aka "The Professor"

Tropical Fish Hobbyist Magazine

Capital Cichlids Associations

Photo Credits

Lawrence Smith

Royalty Free Stock Photos at Fotolia.com

Notes

Notes

Notes

Notes